CONTENTS

1

Slime Time

Deep in the forest, a blob of glistening yellow slime creeps slowly over the surface of a damp, rotting log. This weird organism isn't an alien life form—it's a slime mold. Brightly colored, jelly-like slime molds are among the oddest members of the fungus family, and the only ones that can move.

Slime molds are just one example of the strange shapes and colors of fungi. Some fungi reach enormous sizes. There are puff-ball fungi as big as sheep. A bracket fungus more than 3 feet (1 m) wide and nearly 5 feet (1.5 m) long was found in Washington State. Washington also holds the record for the largest known fungus—a network of caplike mushrooms and underground fibers that covers 1,500 acres! At the other end of the scale are fungi so small they can't be seen without magnification. Some of these, such as the yeasts that make bread rise, are better known for their actions than their looks.

SLIME
MOLDS AND FUNGI

TEXT BY ELAINE PASCOE

PHOTOGRAPHS BY DWIGHT KUHN

BLACKBIRCH PRESS, INC.
WOODBRIDGE, CONNECTICUT

Published by Blackbirch Press, Inc.
260 Amity Road
Woodbridge, CT 06525

To my son, David   To Carey
–D.K.   –E.P.

©1999 by Blackbirch Press, Inc.
Text ©1999 by Elaine Pascoe
Photographs ©1999 by Dwight Kuhn
First Edition

Email: staff@blackbirch.com
Web site: www.blackbirch.com

Printed in the United States

10 9 8 7 6 5 4 3 2

front cover: slime mold plasmodium moving across a rotten log
back cover: (left to right) pretzel mold, witches' butter fungi, tomentella fungi, the fruiting bodies of a slime mold

Library of Congress Cataloging-in-Publication Data
Pascoe, Elaine.
Slime, molds, and fungi / by Elaine Pascoe. — 1st ed.
    p.   cm. — (Nature close-up)
    Includes bibliographical references and index.
    Summary: Using hands-on natural science projects, explores and explains different types and characteristics of fungi.
    ISBN 1-56711-182-3 (lib. bdg. : alk. paper)
    1. Fungi—Juvenile literature. 2. Fungi—Experiments—Juvenile literature. [1. Fungi.
2. Fungi—Experiments. 3. Experiments.] I. Title. II. Series: Pascoe, Elaine. Nature close-up.
QK603.5.P37   1999
579.5—dc21   97-36751
                                           CIP
                                           AC

Note on metric conversions: The metric conversions given in Chapters 2 and 3 of this book are not always exact equivalents of U.S. measures. Instead, they provide a workable quantity for each experiment in metric units. The abbreviations used are:

cm	centimeter	**kg**	kilogram
m	meter	**l**	liter
g	gram	**cc**	cubic centimeter

The fruiting body of a slime mold sits on the moist ground.

Fungi play an important and helpful role in the cycle of life. Many help to break down dead plant and animal material, returning useful nutrients to the soil. Some fungi are also a source of food, for animals and for people. Other fungi are poisonous, and some even cause disease. All, however, are fascinating, and they are unlike any other living things.

Water mold grows on a dead salamander. The mold decomposes the salamander, returning useful nutrients to the pond.

NOT ANIMAL, NOT VEGETABLE

Fungi form one of the five kingdoms of living things. Scientists once considered fungi to be simple plants. Like most plants, most fungi (except slime molds) don't move around. But fungi don't have roots, leaves, flowers, or seeds. And unlike green plants, they can't manufacture their own food. Fungi draw nutrients from their surroundings. When a fungus grows on a rotting log, for example, the log is food for the fungus. The fungus secretes powerful enzymes—chemicals that break down the wood into nutrients that the fungus can absorb and use.

Fungi are found all over the world, on land and in water. Most varieties do best in damp conditions and in warm, but not hot, temperatures. They don't need light, but each kind of fungus needs certain materials for growth. Some grow on dead plant or animal material. Some grow on materials like bread or cheese, which contain ingredients that come from plants and animals. And some grow on living plants or animals. These fungi are considered parasites. Many parasitic fungi cause diseases—for example, athlete's foot and ringworm in people, and various blights in plants.

This series of photographs shows a peach as it is slowly decomposed by molds.

FREAKY FUNGI

Fungi take many colorful shapes, and people often give them colorful common names. Here are a few:

Fairy cups: The fruiting bodies of this fungus are shaped like little cups. When you see them along the edge of a shaded road or path, you might think that someone has littered the ground with bottle caps or buttons.

Witches' butter: This fungus produces jelly-like fruiting bodies that look like glistening globs of butter. It grows on fallen branches and leaves, in damp weather.

Fairy fingers: These pale stalks push up from the ground like ghostly white fingers. They are actually the fruiting bodies of a type of club fungus.

Eyelash: The fruiting body of the eyelash fungus is a cup fringed with tiny fibers—like a set of eyelashes.

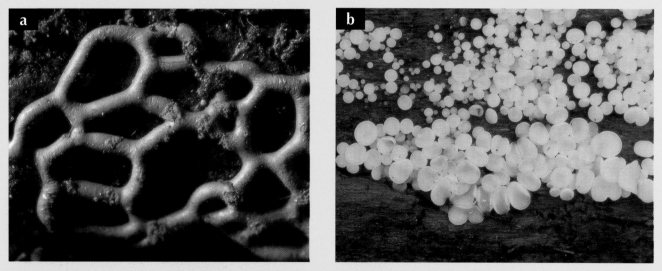

Pretzel slime (a), fairy cups fungi (b), spindle coral slime (c), witches' butter fungi (d), pipe cleaner slime (e), and eyelash fungi (f)

Strange slime: Slime molds take even stranger forms. Coral slime is translucent, with icicle-like projections. Wolf's milk slime forms oozing pink mounds. And although you wouldn't want to eat them, many slime molds look like—and are named for—foods. There's scrambled-egg slime, pretzel slime, tapioca slime, red raspberry slime, and carnival (cotton) candy slime!

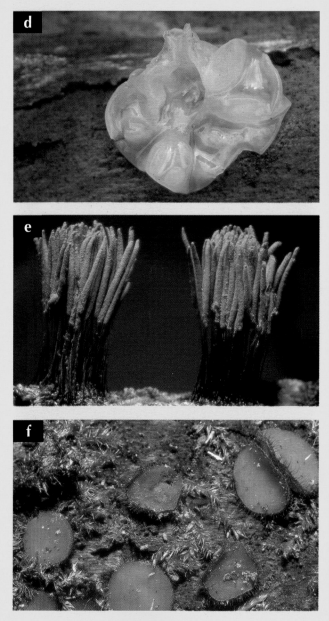

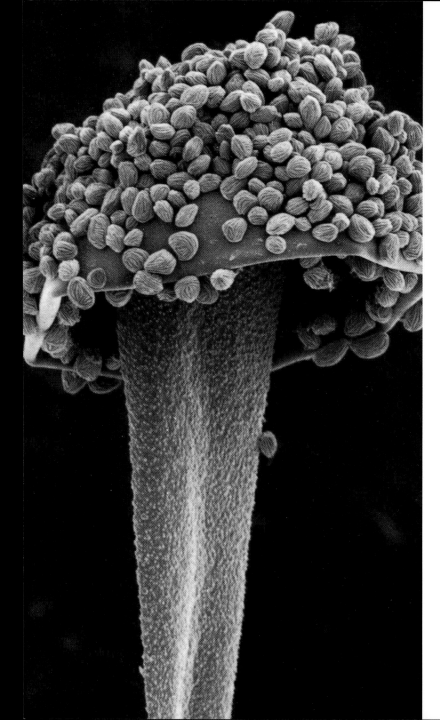

A microscopic image of mold with its top covered in spores

While tiny yeasts are single-celled organisms, most fungi are more complicated. Fungi like the molds that grow on bread and fruit are mainly made up of fine, tangled threads called hyphae. The hyphae form a network called the mycelium. This network secretes enzymes that break down the bread and absorb nutrients from it.

If you were to scrape off a bit of the mold and place it on a new piece of bread or fruit, the mold would keep right on growing, forming a new fungus. But fungi also reproduce in another way. When conditions are right, a bread mold sends up tiny, club-like structures called fruiting bodies. They break open, releasing tiny spores that scatter like dust. Those that land where they find food, warmth, and moisture germinate and form new molds.

Other fungi also reproduce by releasing spores. Methods of forming spores vary, however. For example, the hyphae of some fungi form male or female sex cells. Spores form only after male and female cells unite. Spores sometimes float in the air for years, traveling thousands of miles. Chances are there are some in the air around you right now.

Spindly mold grows on a tomato.

FATAL FUNGI

Only some fungi are edible. Some varieties cause hallucinations, and some are poisonous. The deadliest mushrooms belong to the amanita family. They include some very attractive varieties, such as the white destroying angel and the orange-capped fly amanita. But looks are deceiving. Eating even a piece of a destroying angel can cause death.

It takes an expert to tell edible mushrooms from poisonous mushrooms—and sometimes even experts are fooled. To be safe, eat only mushrooms that are sold in food stores, and NEVER eat any mushrooms you find growing wild.

THE FUNGUS FAMILY

Scientists divide fungi into several groups, based on the way they reproduce and on other characteristics. Here are some of the most interesting kinds.

- **Slime molds:** These strange organisms are usually grouped with fungi, but they are unlike them in many ways. A slime mold's life has two distinct stages. During its feeding stage, the slime mold is a mass of jelly-like living material called protoplasm. It flows slowly over rotting wood, among decaying leaves, or in damp soil. As it creeps along, the slime mold surrounds and feeds on bacteria and other bits of organic materials.

A slime mold plasmodium, as this creeping mass is called, may be white, red, orange, or yellow, depending on the variety of mold. In most types, the plasmodium forms many veins and branches as it flows. When the slime mold is mature, the plasmodium changes. It starts to look more like a fungus, and it sprouts little fruiting bodies that release spores. Slime molds also change when the weather is too dry. From a jelly-like glob, a slime mold thickens into a resting stage. It can survive like this from one month up to a year depending on the species. Slime molds are found all over the world. Some even grow at the edges of melting snow banks on cold mountain tops.

Above: A slime mold plasmodium moves across a rotting log.
Below left: Fruiting bodies of young, immature slime mold
Below right: Fruiting bodies of a mature slime mold

• **Club fungi:** Mushrooms are the most familiar members of this family. Capped mushrooms, like the button mushrooms sold in supermarkets, are actually fruiting bodies. They release spores from gills, located under the "umbrella." A single mushroom can produce about 2 billion spores. The main part of the fungus lives underground, nourished by rotting plant material. Some fungi in this group live in rotting wood, and send out projections that look like brackets or fans.

Other club fungi include puffballs, which burst open to release clouds of spores. Most puffballs are small, but one type grows almost six feet (1.8 meters) across. Stinkhorn fungi give off an odor that attract flies and beetles, which then carry the spores away. Also in this family are various rots and smuts, which cause plant diseases.

Mushrooms are the fruiting bodies of members of the club fungi family.

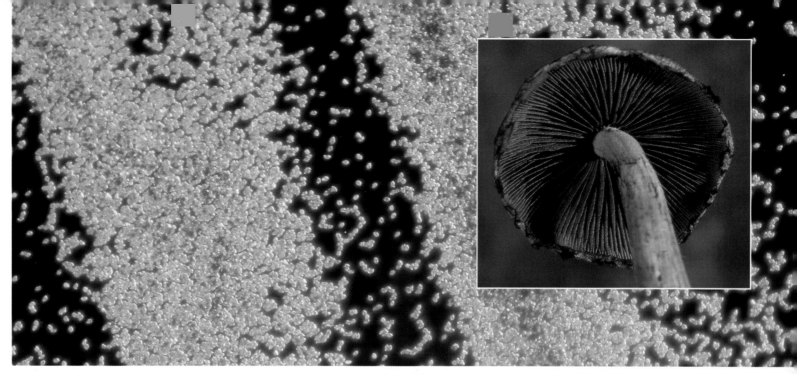

The spore print of a mushroom is seen close-up. *Inset:* The gills underneath a mushroom release reproductive spores.

• **Sac fungi:** Members of the sac fungi group include some highly prized delicacies, such as morels and truffles. Like other members of the group, they form spores in tiny sac-like structures. Truffles, found mostly in Europe, grow underground. Truffle hunters use trained pigs and dogs to sniff them out and dig them up. These gourmet fungi sell for very high prices. Morels look like mushrooms with odd, wrinkled tops. Some other members of this fungi group are shaped like cups.

Single-celled yeasts also belong to this group. When yeasts break down the sugars and starches in plant material, they produce alcohol and carbon dioxide gas. This process is called fermentation, and it is used to produce alcoholic beverages like wine and beer and to make breads rise. Yeasts generally reproduce by budding—a new yeast cell forms on the side of an existing one, and breaks away.

Turk's cap lichens

• **Lichens:** A lichen is really two organisms in one—a fungus joined with blue-green algae, simple one-celled organisms. Lichens can often be seen on rocks and tree trunks. Through a process called photosynthesis, the algae use the energy in sunlight to produce food. They produce enough nutrients for the fungus as well as for themselves, and the fungus shelters them. The word for this type of relationship, in which living things help each other, is symbiosis. Symbiosis allows lichens to survive in harsh conditions, even in the arctic tundra.

Lichens grow extremely slowly. A fast-growing lichen may increase a quarter to half an inch a year. In cold climates, lichens grow even more slowly than that.

There are thousands of fungi that don't fit neatly into any categories. Among them are various molds, such as the black mold that forms on bread.

FUNGI AND PEOPLE

Molds spoil foods, and fungi that grow on crops (some of which are called blights) can be a major problem for farmers. In the 1840's, a type of fungus caused so much damage to Ireland's potato crop that famine resulted. Certain fungi affect people directly. Some of these cause skin infections such as athlete's foot and ringworm. Some cause allergies and respiratory infections. Some of the diseases caused by fungi can be very serious if not treated. For example, fungal spores can infect the lungs, causing an especially dangerous form of pneumonia.

Blight, which is a destructive fungus that destroys plants, grows on a tomato leaf.

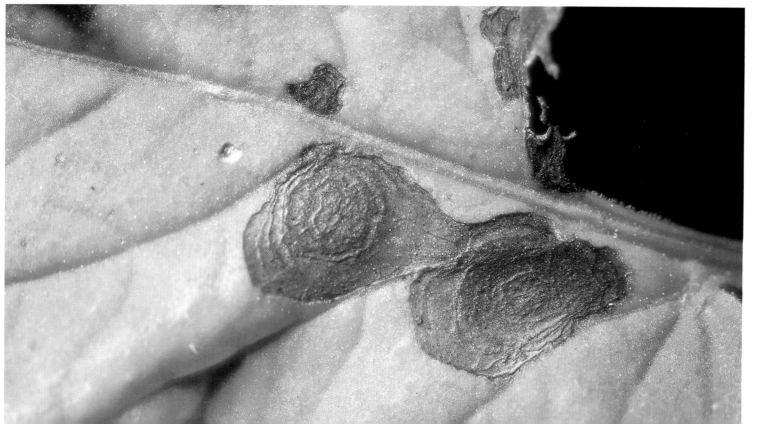

SLIMED!

Was it an invasion from outer space? In 1973, pulsating blobs of bright yellow slime appeared all around Dallas, Texas. Residents panicked as the slime spread. But the "invasion" was only an unusually large appearance of a slime mold, *Fuligo septica*. Besides frightening people, the mold did not harm anything.

Not everyone is disgusted by slime molds. In parts of Mexico, people fry and eat *Fuligo septica* and some other varieties.

Most fungi are not harmful, and people benefit in many ways from them. People have enjoyed eating mushrooms since ancient times. In the 1700's French mushroom-lovers began to grow their favorite varieties in damp caves. Today, raising edible mushrooms is an important industry. The mushrooms are grown indoors, where temperatures and moisture can be controlled.

Another useful fungus is baker's yeast, which is used to make bread. The yeast is mixed with bread dough and allowed to "work," or ferment, producing carbon dioxide and alcohol. When the bread is baked, heat causes bubbles of gas in the dough to expand, puffing up the loaf. The heat also destroys alcohol and kills the yeast. Different types of yeast are used to make alcoholic beverages and other products that depend on fermentation.

Molds are used to make some cheeses and certain vitamins. Perhaps the most helpful fungus in the world is the penicillium mold, a green-gray mold that commonly grows on spoiled fruit. This mold was the original source of penicillin, an antibiotic medicine that has saved countless lives.

Fungi have provided other medicines, in particular other antibiotics, as well. Even slime molds have a use: Scientists study them to learn about protoplasm, the jellylike material that fills living cells and carries out important life functions. All in all, there's a lot to learn from these odd and interesting living things.

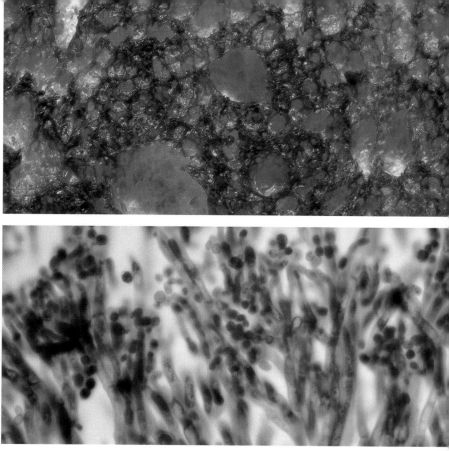

Top: Close-up of bread showing air pockets caused by expanding gas produced from yeast cells
Middle: Microscopic view of penicillium mold
Bottom: Here penicillium is growing on oranges.

2

Collecting and Keeping Fungi and Slime Molds

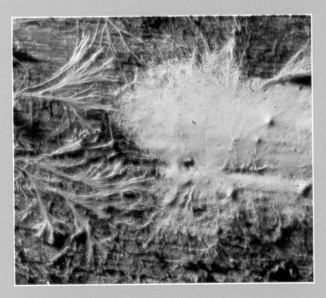

The best way to learn more about fungi and slime molds is to collect samples and study them firsthand. This section will tell you where to look for fungi and slime molds in the wild, how to handle and store them, and how to grow some common molds and mushrooms.

Once you begin to look for them, you'll probably find that fungi are just about everywhere. It's fun to see how many kinds you can find. But because some fungi are poisonous, never eat a mushroom or other fungus that you find. Do not allow the fungi you collect to come in contact with food, and don't leave them where toddlers or pets might find them. Always throw out food on which mold has begun to grow.

HUNTING FOR FUNGI AND SLIME MOLDS

Look for mushrooms, puffballs, and similar fungi outdoors in warm weather. You are most likely to find them in shady spots, where the ground stays slightly moist. Check wooded areas, where a layer of decaying leaves has enriched the soil. Bracket and cup-shaped fungi often grow on damp, rotting wood. Dead trees and fallen branches are the best places to look for them.

**A puffball releases
a cloud of spores.**

Bracket fungus

If you can, collect fungi along with a bit of the material on which they're growing. Use a spoon or a trowel to scoop up some soil with a mushroom, for example, rather than breaking the stem. That way, you will collect some of the thread-like hyphae that lie beneath the soil. Put your mushroom treasures in plastic containers, such as bags or cups. Write down when and where you found each one.

Tree trunks and boulders are good spots to find lichens. Lichens are easily harmed by air pollution, so you are not likely to find them growing in cities, near factories that produce pollution, or along busy roadways. Lichens are best collected by breaking off a bit of the tree bark on which you find them growing. Take only small pieces, so you will not harm the tree. Place them in plastic sandwich bags, and label them.

Look for slime molds a day or so after rain, in spring, summer, and fall. They are not hard to find, once you know where to look for them. Damp, rotting wood provides ideal conditions for these strange organisms. When wood rots, the bark becomes loose and traps moisture. Lift up a piece of bark and check underneath. Piles of damp leaves are another good spot in which to hunt. Lift up the top layer of leaves to look for the molds. Observe the molds where you find them, or collect them in the fruiting body stage. For this, break off a piece of the rotting wood where you find the mold, or take the dead leaf that it's growing on. Put it in a covered plastic container, such as an empty butter container, to avoid damaging the delicate mold. At home, to keep it as a specimen, remove the cover to let it dry out.

A "fuzzy cone" slime mold sprouts from a moist, decaying log.

GROWING SLIME MOLDS

With the help of biological supply companies, you can grow slime molds year-round. Some companies, such as those listed on page 46, sell kits with everything you need, including a bit of dried mold and some rolled oats to serve as food for the slime. Follow the kit's instructions to set up your slime mold culture. Then watch as the slime mold plasmodium revives and begins to creep toward the food.

Slime mold plasmodium moves toward a food source.

A pumpkin is enveloped by mold.

GROWING MOLDS

Mold spores are in the air all the time. To grow common molds, all you need to do is provide the food, moisture, and temperatures that these fungi need. It won't take long for mold spores to land on the home you've provided, and they'll quickly begin to grow.

Many people are allergic to molds and mold spores. For that reason, it's a good idea to keep your mold-growing containers covered. Use throwaway containers, such as sealable plastic sandwich bags or recycled baby food jars or butter containers covered with plastic wrap. When you are finished with your experiments and observations, throw the entire container away.

BREAD MOLD: GROWING ONE OF THE MOST COMMON MOLDS

What to Do:
1. Place a piece of fresh bread in a clean, empty butter container or a sealable plastic bag.
2. Sprinkle a few drops of water on the bread, or mist it lightly, or put a piece of slightly damp paper towel under it.
3. Leave the bread exposed to the air for about 30 minutes.

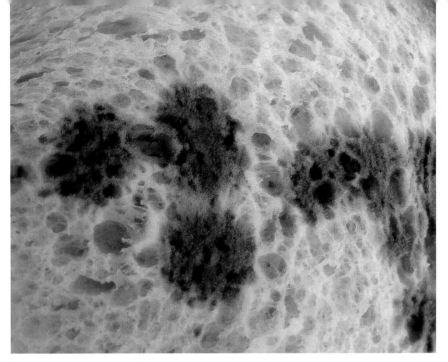

4. Cover the container with plastic wrap, secured with a rubber band (or seal the plastic bag, leaving a tiny opening to allow some air to circulate).

5. Place the container in a dark place at room temperature. After a few days, start checking for mold growth. Once mold starts to grow, don't open the container.

Penicillium mold: The green-gray mold that is the source of the antibiotic penicillin is also common. To grow it, follow the steps under "Bread mold," but use a piece of lemon instead of bread.

GROWING MUSHROOMS

You can grow edible mushrooms using kits available through mail-order suppliers. (See page 46 for some sources). These kits include a plastic-lined growing box, peat moss, and compost (decayed plant material) that has been sterilized to kill harmful organisms. The compost has been "seeded" with mushroom spawn.

To start the mushrooms growing, cover the compost with moistened peat moss. Put the plastic liner over the top, and close the box. Put the box in a warm place, out of direct sunlight.

You can get mushroom-growing kits from many mail-order sources. *Inset:* Close-up of mushroom spawn growing on the specially prepared compost mixture.

Above: After 10 to 15 days, moistened moss will show signs of growth.
Right: Within another week or two, the threads will grow into full-blown fruiting bodies.

In 10 to 15 days, the surface of the peat moss should be covered with gray threads of fungus. Then the top of the box is raised, so fruiting bodies—mushrooms—can form. Put the box where the temperature is 55 to 65 degrees F (13 to 18 degrees C) and mist the peat moss lightly with water to keep it slightly damp. The mushrooms should start to grow in a week or two.

31

3

Investigating Slime Molds and Other Types of Fungi

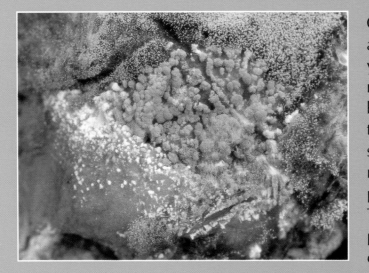

On the pages that follow, you'll find some activities and experiments that will help you find out more about fungi and slime molds. Have fun with these activities, but take some precautions. Remember that some people are allergic to mold spores. To avoid spreading spores, keep molds in covered containers. Use disposable containers whenever you can. Then, when you have finished an experiment, throw away the materials, container and all.

WHERE ARE SLIME MOLDS MOST LIKELY TO GROW?

Many slime molds grow on tree bark and dead leaves. Is one bit of bark as good as another to the molds, or do they prefer certain types? Decide what you think, and then try to grow some of these odd molds to find out.

What to Do:

1. Collect several different kinds of bark—smooth bark, rough bark, bark from pines or other evergreens, and bark from trees that lose their leaves in fall. A field guide will help identify the trees. Pry off only small pieces of bark. Put each sample in a separate plastic bag, and label it.

2. At home, transfer your samples to clean plastic containers. Place a piece of paper towel in each container, and place a bark sample on it. Add enough water to completely cover the bark. Cover the containers with plastic wrap, secured with rubber bands, and label.

What You Need:

* Samples of different tree barks, each about 2 inches (5 centimeters) across
* Plastic sandwich bags and a tool, such as a butter knife, for collecting the bark
* A disposable plastic container, such as a recycled butter container, for each bark sample
* Paper towels
* Distilled or clean tap water
* Plastic wrap
* Rubber bands

3. After 24 hours, pour off the water. Make sure the bark samples are positioned rough side up, and cover the containers again. Put them in a place where they will be at room temperature, and out of direct sunlight.

4. Check each day to see if slime molds have begun to grow in any of the containers. Slime molds vary in size and appearance. Some fruiting bodies are smaller than the letters on this page. A magnifying glass will help you check the bark. Be patient—slime molds can take weeks to develop. Always replace the cover of your containers after checking. If the paper towels start to dry out, mist the contents lightly with clean water.

Results: Keep a record of slime molds that grow in your containers. Note when they appear and what they look like.

Conclusion: Which samples produced the most slime? Which produced the least? Repeat this activity with different materials—dead leaves, bits of rotting wood, or hay.

ON WHICH FOODS DO MOLDS GROW BEST?

Mold spores are everywhere, but they can't begin to grow until they land where conditions are right. What kinds of food provide the best conditions for molds? Make a prediction based on what you have read about these fungi. This experiment will help you find out if you are right.

What to Do:

1. Arrange pieces of the various foods in your container. Mist them lightly and evenly with water or place slightly misted paper towel under them.
2. Leave the container uncovered for about 30 minutes. Then cover it with plastic wrap, secured with a rubber band. Place it in a warm, dark place.
3. After a couple of days, begin checking for mold growth. Check each day, and write down what you see. When you are finished with your observations, throw the unopened container away.

What You Need:
* A variety of foods—bread, dry toast, breakfast cereal, cheese, and slices of tomato, carrot, lemon, kiwi, or other fruits
* A tin pie plate or other disposable container
* Plastic wrap and a rubber band to cover the container
* Plain water in a spray bottle

Results: Compare the amount of mold that has grown on each food. Are the molds all the same, or are there different types?

Conclusion: Which foods grew the most mold? What qualities do those foods have?

HOW DOES TEMPERATURE AFFECT YEAST GROWTH?

When baker's yeast is mixed with bread dough, it starts to break down the dough. In the process, it produces bubbles of carbon dioxide gas that give bread a light, spongy texture. Like other fungi, yeasts thrive in certain conditions. This experiment will help you find out what temperatures yeasts like best. Before you start, make a prediction based on what you know about these helpful and commonly used one-celled fungi.

What to Do:

1. Measuring carefully, mix 1/2 cup water with 3 teaspoons of sugar and 3 teaspoons of dry yeast. Pour the mixture into the bottle. (Do this over a sink. A funnel will help.)

What You Need:

* Dry baker's yeast (sold in supermarkets)
* Sugar
* Water
* A narrow-mouthed bottle, such as a 16-ounce plastic soda bottle
* A large container, big enough to hold the bottle
* A balloon
* Strong tape, such as black electrical tape
* Rubber bands
* Cup and teaspoon measures, and a measuring tape

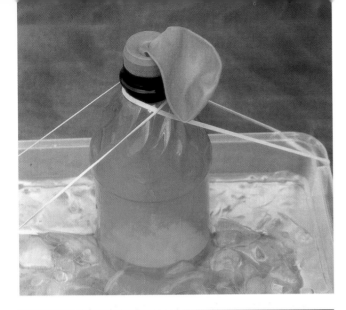

2. Cover the container with the balloon, stretching the opening over the bottle's mouth. Tape the balloon securely to the bottle neck.

3. Place the container in a warm room and check it every hour. If conditions are right, the yeast cells will multiply. As they produce carbon dioxide gas, the balloon will start to expand. Measure the circumference of the balloon (the distance around it) and record the measurement each time you check.

4. Repeat the experiment, but this time put the bottle in a warm water bath. For this, put warm water in the second container. Refill the bottle with a fresh yeast/sugar mixture, using the same measurements, and stand it in the warm water. If the bottle tips, use rubber bands to keep it upright. Check hourly and record your observations, as before.

5. Repeat the experiment again, this time using cold water and ice in the water bath. Once again, refill the bottle with a fresh yeast/sugar mixture. Stand it in the cold bath and record your observations.

Results: Which balloon grew biggest and fastest?
Conclusion: What do your results tell you about the best temperatures for yeasts?
You can vary this experiment. For example, use only yeast and water and no sugar. How do your results differ?

HOW DOES YEAST AFFECT DECAY?

In nature, yeasts are often found in plant leaves and fruit, as well as in the soil. They are among the fungi that play a role in the process of decay. How do yeasts affect decay? This activity will help you find out.

What to Do:

1. Put the two banana slices in the container. Sprinkle dry yeast on one.
2. Cover the container with plastic wrap, secured with rubber bands.
3. Put the container in a warm, dark place. Check in a few days to see what is happening to the banana slices. Discard the unopened container when you are done with your observations.

Results: Compare the two banana slices. Which shows more signs of decay? Signs include softening, runniness, and discoloration.

Conclusion: Based on your results, how would you describe the role yeasts play in decay? Try this experiment again, using different kinds of fruit, and see if your results are the same.

What You Need:
* Two banana slices
* A clean disposable container, such as a paper plate or butter container
* Plastic wrap and a rubber band to cover the container
* Dry yeast

MORE FUN WITH FUNGI

1. Make a mushroom spore print. All mushrooms release spores through gills, slit-like openings on the underside of the cap. Different varieties of mushrooms have different gill patterns and spore colors. Spore prints are like fungus fingerprints, showing the differences. Here's how to make one:

• Collect a full-grown mushroom, with the cap fully expanded. Cut off the stem below the cap.

• Place the mushroom, gills down, on a sheet of paper. Put a bowl, a glass, or another container over it, and leave it overnight. Be careful not to move or disturb the mushroom once it is on the paper.

• In the morning, carefully remove the bowl and the mushroom. Spores will have fallen out of the gills onto the paper, creating a pattern. Be careful not to breathe on them, or they'll blow away. Collect other kinds of mushrooms, and compare the colors and patterns of their spores.

Plasmodium feeding stage of slime mold on damp rotted wood

2. Find out how fast slime mold moves. Find a slime mold on damp rotted wood. If it is in the feeding stage, don't collect it or disturb it. Instead, put a push pin into the wood at (but not in) the forward edge of the creeping slime. Check daily to see how far the slime mold has traveled in relation to the pin. Come back later to see the fruiting body stage.

3. Go on a fungus hunt. Search your yard, nearby woods, or a park to see how many different kinds of fungi you can find. Look for mushrooms, bracket fungi, and molds. Check plants for powdery mildew, which looks like white dust on leaves. You may even find mold and mildew growing on your house. Take along a magnifying glass to view the fungi in detail. Make a record of each type you find, noting when and where you saw it. Do some places have more fungi than others? Can you think of reasons why they might?

You can hunt mushrooms just about anywhere. Look for moist, shaded, and wooded conditions. (Remember: Never handle or eat any wild mushrooms.)

A fly is slowly consumed by a parasitic fungus.

4. Fungi are everywhere—even in places you'd never think to look. If you find a dead fly, take a close look at it with a magnifying glass. A type of fungus attacks and kills flies, so you may see fungal growth on the body.

43

RESULTS AND CONCLUSIONS

Here are some possible outcomes to the activities on pages 33 to 39. You may not get the same results. Many factors affect the way fungi grow and behave. If your outcomes differ, think about the possible reasons. What do you think led to your results? Repeat the activity and see if the outcome is the same.

Where Are Slime Molds Most Likely to Grow?

Slime molds are most likely to appear on rough bark, which has lots of hiding places for mold spores. They rarely grow on the bark of pines and other evergreens.

On Which Foods Do Molds Grow Best?

Moist foods, such as soft fruits, generally provide the best conditions for molds. You may see several different types of mold in your container, depending on what spores were floating in the air when you set up your experiment.

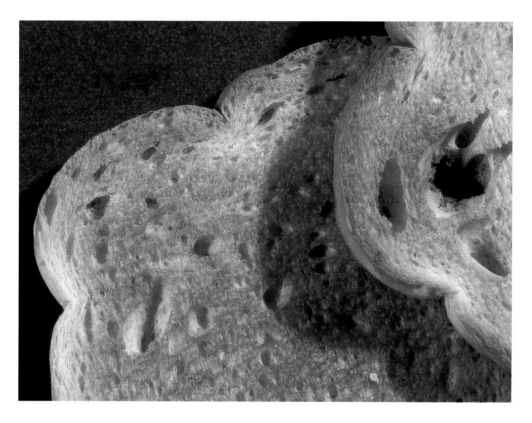

Baker's yeast is used to make bread.

How Does Temperature Affect Yeast Growth?

Baker's yeast grows well in warm temperatures, between 75 and 85 degrees Fahrenheit (24 and 30 degrees Celsius). Cold temperatures will slow or halt growth and hot temperatures will kill the yeast cells.

How Does Yeast Affect Decay?

Yeast speeds the decay process by breaking down sugars and starches in plant material. You will probably find that the banana slice with yeast decayed more quickly than the slice without.

SOME WORDS ABOUT FUNGI

antibiotic A medicine that fights bacterial infections.

enzymes Substances that prompt or speed up chemical changes, such as those that occur when food is digested. All living things produce enzymes of many kinds.

germinate Begin to grow.

organic Living or derived from living things.

parasite A living thing that lives on or in another, getting food from its host without giving any benefit in return.

symbiosis A relationship in which living things depend on each other for food and other needs.

SOURCES FOR FUNGI-RELATED SUPPLIES

The following companies sell mushroom-growing kits and other fungi-related supplies through the mail.

Carolina Biological Supply
2700 York Road
Burlington, NC 27215
1-800-33405551

Connecticut Valley Biological
82 Valley Road
PO Box 326
Southampton, MA 01073
1-800-628-7748

FURTHER READING

Jackson, Ellen. *The Book of Slime.* Brookfield, CT: Millbrook Press, 1997.

Madgwick, Wendy. *Fungi and Lichens.* Chatham, NJ: Raintree Steck-Vaughn, 1990.

Margulis, Lynn. *Diversity of Life: The Five Kingdoms.* Springfield, NJ: Enslow, 1992.

Silverstein, Alvin, Virginia, and Robert. *Fungi.* New York: Twenty-First Century Books, 1996.

Tesar, Jenny. *Fungi.* Woodbridge, CT: Blackbirch Press, 1994.

INDEX

Note: Page numbers in italics indicate pictures.